ROUAULT
FUJIMURA

Soliloquies

ROUAULT FUJIMURA

Soliloquies

Thomas S Hibbs

with a refraction by Makoto Fujimura

Square Halo Books

THE EXHIBITION *ROUAULT-FUJIMURA: SOLILOQUIES* WAS MADE POSSIBLE WITH THE SUPPORT OF THE FOUNDATION GEORGES ROUAULT. SPECIAL THANKS TO THE FOUNDATION FOR PERMISSION TO REPRINT ROUAULT'S PAINTINGS IN THIS BOOK.

First Edition 2009

Copyright ©2009 Square Halo Books
P.O. Box 18954, Baltimore, MD 21206
ISBN-13: 978-0-9785097-2-9
ISBN-10: 0-9785097-2-2

Printed in the U.S.A.

For a long time I had been
turning over within myself
many different things,
and for many days I had been
assiduously seeking my very self
and what was good for me
(or, if you will,
what evil I should avoid),
when suddenly it spoke to me.
I know not whether
it was I myself or
something else outside
or inside of me;
for this is precisely what I am
struggling mightily to know.

—Saint Augustine

At the end of 2009 the Dillon Gallery hosted an exhibit featuring works of art from Georges Rouault and Makoto Fujimura, titled "Soliloquies." A paradoxical title indeed! Etymologically, a soliloquy is a "speech alone." As we know from the plays of Shakespeare, most famously *Hamlet* and *Macbeth,* the precondition of a soliloquy is a stage that is empty except for the presence of the speaker. To pair soliloquies, then, seems odd. But a soliloquy is not a monologue, in which the expectation is that there will be only one speaker. Even in a play, a soliloquy is but one speech among many—other soliloquies, speeches before crowds, and dialogues with a varying number of participants. Rouault

Fujimura *Soliloquies—Joy.* 64 x 80 inches.
Rouault *Paysan a la moisson.* 12.4 x 19 inches.

gave the title *Soliloquies* to a book he composed about his art; Fujimura's
selection of this title for the exhibit was a sign of his debt to Rouault.

The very notion of a soliloquy dates back to the fourth-century
work of Augustine, who coined the term as the title from one of his
earliest books, in the year 386, as he made his final transition from
paganism to Christianity. As he comments in that work, "Because
we are speaking with ourselves alone, I want the book to be called
The Soliloquies." In the course of his internal dialogue, Augustine
states that the soliloquy is a speech that involves internal dialogue (a
searching within the self to uncover the truth or decide upon a course
of action) as well as the potential inclusion of others as listeners and
perhaps even as potential dialogue partners. As the opening quotation
from Augustine indicates, a soliloquy involves an internal searching, a
recognition that the self is a mystery to itself, a mystery whose
depths can be plumbed by "questioning."

8

The internal struggle to speak through art is central to Rouault's
understanding of his vocation. In contrast to Matisse, who said he
would cease painting if no one else would ever see the fruits of his
labor, Rouault said, "Of course I would go on; I would have need of that
spiritual dialogue." This does not, however, mean that the communication with and to others is irrelevant. As Fujimura has said, that although
painting is often seen "... as a solitary act in a studio, creativity is sharp-
ened by collaborative process. Art is never born in a vacuum."

The title also captures the roots of artistic creation in silence.
Rouault once observed, "Solitude is the natural dwelling place of all
thought." Communication of the most powerful emotions, the deepest
truths, and most unfathomable mysteries of our condition presup-
poses a meditative silence—even a solitude of spirit.

In our current cultural context, soliloquy serves another end. It engages, without succumbing to any of it, the tendency in the world of art to reduce artistic creativity to self-expression, to the eccentric and the idiosyncratic, or even to a celebration of what is offensive. The problem with much of contemporary art is that, even as it laments our alienation, it just reproduces the solipsism at the level of art. Fujimura comments:

Rouault *Hiver pauvre village*. 7 x 14 inches.

The main cause of this corruption, or the pollution in the
aesthetic river of culture, is self-aggrandizement and a type
of embezzlement made in the name of advancing the creative
arts . . .. We pollute the cultural landscape with irresponsible

Fujimura *Soliloquies—Passion.* 64 x 80 inches.
Rouault *Christ.* 26.38 x 18.90 inches.

expressions in the name of progress and call them freedom of speech. Thus, our cultural landscape is increasingly uninhabitable. If we cannot dwell inside the imaginative landscape of what is offered, then what is the purpose of creativity?

Yet the fragmentary character of our language about the beautiful and the ugly is a reality that cannot simply be bypassed in an effort to produce unity and clarity. Because it begins from the articulation of a personal vision and moves outward in the hope of dialogue, the soliloquy meets us where we are. It acknowledges our difficulty in establishing a common language—a basis for communication across the multifarious discourses of modern life.

"Soliloquies" also befits an exhibit of the art of two outsiders who work at the margins of the mainstream movements and who find themselves between or at the margins of well-known trends. Stylistically and thematically, Rouault has always been difficult to characterize. Fujimura's integration of Japanese and Western artistic styles makes him similarly eccentric with respect to the standard categories. Both deploy a method often associated with abstraction, yet neither is precisely an abstract artist.

Pairing soliloquies indicates that every soliloquy is potentially a dialogue. For Augustine, Rouault, and Fujimura, the soliloquy is an internal conversation, but one that is not closed in upon itself; rather it is open to others and to the world. The particular set of soliloquies allows viewers to engage each artist on his own terms and in relation to the other. We are certainly invited to discern the influence of Rouault on Fujimura, but what about the reverse? "True influence is catalytic," says Fujimura. Insofar as the soliloquists are living voices,

12

the juxtaposition of the two allows us to rethink Rouault, to notice features of his work we had not before. At least for viewers, influence is catalytic in more than one direction.

A Forgotten Mainstream

Born in 1871 just outside Paris, in a part of the city devastated by war, Rouault trained in his teens in a workshop that produced stained glass. By 1891, he was a pupil of Gustave Moreau and enrolled in the Ecole des Beaux-Arts in Paris, where he was a classmate of Matisse. After

Rouault *Hiver.* 7 x 14 inches.

the death of his teacher in 1898, Rouault endured great difficulty, not just through financial strain but also as an outsider. Additionally, Rouault suffered a violent psychological upheaval, the artistic result being that he "began to paint with an outrageous lyricism which disconcerted everybody."

Makoto Fujimura was born in 1960 in Boston and was educated biculturally in the United States and Japan, receiving a bachelor's

15

degree from Bucknell and a master's degree from Tokyo National
University of Fine Arts. His work combines "the medieval technique
of Japanese painting, loosely now called Nihonga, with the metaphysi-
cal concerns of the early twentieth century and medieval European
works." He founded the International Arts Movement, a fellowship
of artists that describes itself as "wrestling with the deep issues of art,
faith and humanity."

Rouault *Paysage d'Automne Avec Trois personnages.* 12.6 x 16 inches.
Fujimura *La fin au-dela #1.* 9 x 12 inches.

Neither artist is easy to classify. They work between or at the margins of mainstream trends in art: Rouault between the Fauvist stylistic experimentalism and the traditional art of the craftsmen of the medieval cathedrals, and Fujimura between Eastern and Western, between modernist abstraction and classical Japanese methods. What their ultimate legacies will be is unclear. This is understandable in the case of a living artist such as Fujimura. He is increasingly receiving recognition both in the United States and in Japan. Rouault, however, remains an enigma a half-century after his death. In some quarters, he is ranked among the masters of twentieth-century art. Yet his work remains oddly underappreciated. American interest in Rouault was high in the years immediately after his death in 1958 at the age of 86, with a major Museum of Modern Art exhibit. But not much more than
a decade later, interest declined and remained dormant into

16

this century. There are signs of a reawakening of interest, with a number of impressive exhibits in the last decade.

The Dillon Gallery exhibit has added an important dimension to the current reappraisal of Rouault, precisely by the juxtaposition of Rouault's work with that of a contemporary artist who claims him as an influence. There are, of course, many differences between the two artists, both in terms of their lineage, artistry, subject matter, and style. The scale of Fujimura's paintings is much larger than that of Rouault's; Rouault is much more actively engaged than is Fujimura with the Western tradition of portrait painting. About the exhibit, Fujimura himself has observed, "Rouault and my paintings are vastly different, and yet share a common interest in the process of painting, color, approach." Beyond color and palette, there is the similar interest in the painting of landscape, as both a shared subject matter and a

shared source of spiritual reflection. Fujimura sees Rouault as the first twenty-first century painter, someone who was "using the language of a secular age to explain a sacred calling." Teasing out these similarities is the task of "Soliloquies."

There is an interesting and little-known precedent for linking Rouault to an artist of Japanese descent. Nowhere outside France has Rouault's work been more appreciated or exhibited than in Japan. Artists and collectors in Japan came to know Rouault's work in the 1920s, and by 1934 his stature earned him a major exhibit by the

Rouault *Scene paysannes.* 16 x 23 inches.

Fukishima Collection at the Nihon Theater in Tokyo. His early training in stained glass, his physical use of color, and his deployment of
abstraction as a means of moving the viewer to apprehend the spiritual realities latent in the painting—all this endeared him to Japanese

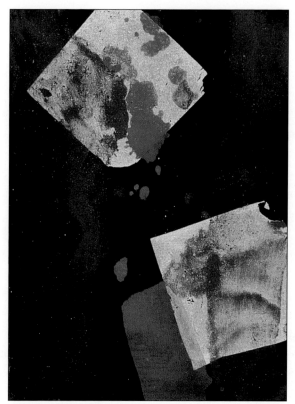

artists and viewers.

One striking similarity between Rouault and the contemporary Japanese-American artist Fujimura is their dialectical relationship to traditions that have fallen into desuetude, in both cases pre-modern traditions. Fujimura himself has drawn connections between the Eastern traditions that have informed his work and the Western medieval traditions that helped shape Rouault's vision. Rouault confessed

Rouault *Automne*. 7.4 x 5.4 inches.
Fujimura *La fin au-dela #2*. 9 x 12 inches.

that he did not feel he belonged "to this modern life" but to the "age of the cathedrals."

In both cases, an early training in pre-modern methods and artistic visions is later brought into conversation with modern methods of art and the contemporary questions of meaning. Thus, the traditionalism in the art of Roualt and Fujimura embodies a more complicated relationship to the past than that of mere repetition. Precisely because they have not been enmeshed in any particular school or movement of art, they have been able to discern the way in which neglected resources from the past could be brought to bear on the predicament of art in the contemporary age.

Indeed, the enduring Romantic conception of the artist as involved principally in self-expression combines with the assumption that worthy art is always engaged in novel forms of protest against established order. This results in the perception of art as negative, parasitic, and ephemeral. In such a context, we lose the ability to distinguish better from worse, advance from regress, enduring excellence from evanescent popularity. E.H. Gombrich notes in his magisterial *Story of Art* that self-expression became the motive for art only after it had lost all other purposes.

In an age when the artistic process is reduced to self-expression and when creativity is reduced to mere novelty, it might seem surprising to find artists embracing the medieval notion of artistic training as apprenticeship and arguing for a link between creativity and tradition.

As the influential contemporary philosopher Alasdair MacIntyre has argued, it is only by participation in a living tradition that one can understand what it means to make progress. In stark contrast to

the notion of tradition as static, repetitious, and unreflective, living traditions are sites of development, intelligible novelty, and ongoing debates about excellence.

Outsiders, working at the margins, can paradoxically provide an avenue for the recovery of tradition, of ancient forms of art and meditative practice long forgotten by mainstream artists. Another paradox: true creativity must have its roots in an appreciation of the achievements of the past. Our connection to the tradition is broken, and re-establishing tradition is not a matter of simply asserting our fidelity to it. As T. S Eliot put it in his influential essay, "Tradition and the Individual Talent," the artist must have a sense not only of the

Rouault *Village Aux arbes morts*. 12.7 x 17 inches.

"pastness of the past but also of its presence."

Standing outside the mainstream, both Rouault and Fujimura re-appropriate traditions neglected, in some cases scorned, by the dominant trends in art. The re-appropriation and extension of tradition allows not only for a recovery of what had been lost but also for envisioning something new in the tradition, for the realization of

unanticipated possibilities latent within the tradition.

Given their angular approach to tradition, the art of outsiders is as likely to provoke among the advocates of tradition as much befuddle-ment or distress as affirmation. Rouault's art provoked what William Dyrness calls "pious rage." Fellow Catholic Leon Bloy accused Rouault of being able only "to imagine the most atrocious and avenging

Rouault *Paysage Africain (aux trois barques)*. 16 x 18.4 inches.
Fujimura *La fin au-dela #7*. 11 x 14 inches.

Fujimura *Soliloquies—Grace.* 64 x 80 inches.
Rouault *Christ (Passion)*

caricatures" and being "attracted exclusively by the ugly." But Bloy misses what is deeply traditional in Rouault's deployment of disfigurement. As Pierre Courthion, a friend of Rouault and author of the magisterial *Rouault,* suggests, "I see him as more closely related to the artists of the cathedral sculptures and to the distortions, deformities, and comic effects that they nestled in the niches beneath their tympana."

Of course, one of the goals of the craftsmen of the cathedrals was to build works of art that would stand the test of time. Here we confront another paradox. Contemporary artists, more concerned about celebrity status than the anonymous craftsmen of the Old World, have significantly lower ambitions. Remaining in contact with the vital tradition of art can help restore art to its lofty aspirations. This is confirmed in Fujimura's marvelous essay "Fra Angelico and the Five-Hundred-Year Question." Fujimura begins by recounting a trip he made to the Metropolitan Museum in New York to see a Fra Angelico exhibit. Overwhelmed by the initial experience, he retreated from the museum and began to ponder not just why we do not make art like this any longer but also why artists do not even aspire to create art that will endure 500 years. As an apprentice in a medieval workshop, Fra Angelico discovered his artistic "gift" within "the long lasting tradition of art." Where, Fujimura wonders, can a young artist gain such training, not just in techniques but also in the noble aspirations of the artist?

27

Action, Abstraction, and Nature

About the influence of Rouault on this set of Fujimura paintings, Valerie Dillon observed, "Fujimura is using a palette that Rouault used from his stain-glass training: Inky blacks, heavy lines with Jewel tones, and strong forceful colors. Fujimura is starting from a black background and then adding the jewel tones, in homage to Rouault." The catalytic influence of palette and heavy lines helps us discern not only Rouault's impact on Fujimura but also the way in which colors and patterns of images dominate so many of Rouault's canvases. Rouault's human figures often seem to be features of the landscape itself. The juxtaposition, at first quite jarring, of Rouault's images of a crucified Christ with Fujimura's less easily distinguished colors and lines reveals, upon closer examination, influences both stylistic and spiritual.

In the context of the set of paintings on display in this exhibit, it is difficult to resist using the term "abstraction." Hesitant to accept the abstractionist label sometimes placed on his art, Fujimura nonetheless embraces some of its aims. In a *New Yorker* review of the Guggenheim's ambitious 1996 retrospective of abstract art ("Abstraction in the Twentieth Century: Total Risk, Freedom, Discipline"), critic Calvin Tomkins observed that "abstraction did not lead to the promised land of new truths and new freedoms" that lay beyond the limits of representation. Fujimura himself is not as pessimistic about the twentieth century turn to abstraction. He cites Rothko and Gorky as influences whose use of abstraction was an honest attempt to "grapple" with "invisible reality." Yet he remains concerned about the way abstraction can become a kind

29

Fujimura *Twin Rivers of Tamagawa.* 71 x 71 inches.

of gnosticism that repudiates or neglects the material conditions of art. The preoccupation with the physical character of the work of art points up another similarity between Rouault and Fujimura.

Rouault once wrote, "I believe that I have matter, true matter"; his greatest struggles were not mental but rather "battles of technique and material means ..." Perhaps because they both were trained as craftsmen, they cannot forget the physical conditions of making. Etienne Gilson aptly comments:

> One of the main reasons painters find it so hard to make themselves understood when they speak of their art is that their hearers listen with their minds only, not with their hands. If it is a question of painting, the artist himself can form no clear notion of his own art without including in it manual skill.

The attention to the manual conditions of art means that Fujimura and Rouault do not conceive of techniques and forms as neutral. Great artists unite form and content.

Fujimura's Japanese training in the tradition of Nihonga focused on the creative use of malachite, azurite, and materials mixed with animal skin glue (Nikawa). Fujimura associates these techniques 31 with those of classical fresco painting and medieval manuscript illumination. In a marvelous essay on Rouault's process of painting, Jean-Marie Teze calls Rouault an "action painter." After the death of Moreau, he altered his methods and his primary materials. "He laid out patches of color without restraint, applied brush strokes with great pressure . . . lively, flowing, rapid, scalding strokes." The fascination with color was nothing new; in fact, it dates to his time working in the stained glass factory, where he learned to appreciate the "flamboyant reds, golden yellows, ultramarines like those of early antiquity."

Similarly, Fujimura is taken with the materiality of his paintings and with vibrant color. He carefully prepares materials, grinding pigments and laying sheets of gold or silver foil onto paper. Distinguishing the effect of his painting on the viewer from both the

Renaissance accentuation of depth through perspective and the modernist accentuation on surface space, he compares his effect to that of the stained-glass window. He uses what he calls a "semi-transparent layering effect that traps light in the space created between the pigments and between layers of gold or silver foil."

Another way in which abstraction is curtailed or qualified in both painters has to do with the decisive role of landscapes in their art. In terms of the subject matters painted by Rouault and Fujimura, landscapes are the chief point of overlap in what is otherwise a quite different selection of subject matters. No mere reproductions or copies of natural settings, their landscape paintings nonetheless embody a higher realism about nature, one that arises from a silent communing with nature that is also fostered in its viewers. Fujimura's description of Rimpa, a seventeenth-century decorative screen tradition,

applies in large measure to much of his own art: "The Rimpa tradition combines decorative elements of patterns of nature into extravagantly rich images of gold, silver, mineral pigments, and sumi ink." Rouault described landscapes as his "spring-board," which will "always be the basis" of his work. In their attention to landscapes, both Rouault and Fujimura open new artistic paths traceable neither to classical realism nor to impressionism. Indeed, Rouault's approach to nature helped his friend Jacques Maritain, the famous follower of Thomas Aquinas, to re-articulate the scholastic axiom that art imitates nature. He came to repudiate the notion that art merely re-presented what nature had already presented: "Nature was not a model to be slavishly copied."

As already noted, Fujimura worries about the tendency of abstraction toward a gnosticism or Platonism that would render physical reality at best a shadow world and at worst an illusion:

33

Rouault *Fin d'Automne*. 25.2 x 36 inches.
Fujimura *Soliloquies—Passion Study*. 11 x 14 inches.

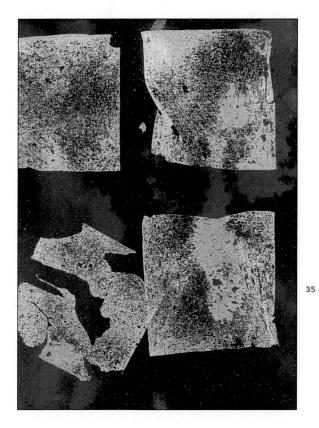

35

"I want my work to be a stripping off the unnecessary while it accen-
tuates the physicality of . . . the textures, colors and materials of the
natural world." He describes the process of producing some of his
best work as akin to the performance art of Jackson Pollock:

> Instead of painting with the paper on the wall, putting on
> the materials with brushes and allowing them to drip, I am

Rouault *Jesus sera en agonie jusqu'a la fin du mond*
Fujimura *La fin au-dela #8*. 9 x 12 inches.

laying the painting surface out horizontally, parallel to the floor, and moving the paint around by lifting one side or the other. It is almost a performance. You have to watch the paint dry and direct the way it forms areas of color by lifting the work in the right way.

The sense of the painting as an ongoing project was dear to Rouault, who "stuck doggedly with a painting in order to achieve, by a process of sedimentation, a material density and richness" and "brought to canvasses a new material color," which critics called "phosphorescence."

Fujimura's use of materials that alter over time underscores the temporality not just of art but also of nature itself. For Fujimura, the incomplete character of the work of art—its mutability over time, and its failure to instantiate fully what it depicts—is part of the essence of art. He quotes Togyu Okamura, a Nihonga painter: "What matters is not how finished the work looks, but how unfinished it remains."

The Art of Attention

The unfinished character of art is an invitation to the viewer to participate in the work itself. The epochs of Rouault and Fujimura are both characterized by political and spiritual crisis, one of the chief symptoms of which is "amnesia" about the animating ideals of human life. One of the goals of the art of Rouault and Fujimura is to cultivate in viewers the art of remembering. The experience of viewing their art

is meditative, if not prayerful.

In his *Story of Art,* Gombrich notes that landscape painting in the East, first in China and then in Japan, was intended to foster a certain "kind of meditation." One might take any object in nature and deploy

Rouault *Passion*

it so as to prompt concentrated mental and spiritual exercise. One might ponder water, for example, "to learn from it, how humble it is, how it yields and yet wears away solid rock, how it is clear and cool and soothing and gives life to the thirsting fields," or mountains to see "how strong and lordly they are, and yet how good, for they allow the

Fujimura *Soliloquies—Genesis.* 64 x 80 inches.
Rouault *Pysage aytomne avec trois personnages*

trees to grow on them."

Similarly, the tradition of stained glass and iconography out of which Rouault works also has a meditative purpose, in which the image is a medium for an encounter between the visible and the invisible. The beginning and end of art, the nourishing conditions of its production and the hoped-for effect on the viewer, mirror one another. On the one hand, the artist's work arises out of silent receptivity to nature and the human condition; on the other, the work produced seeks to foster in viewers a similar soliloquy, a searching within and beyond the work itself. Here the goals of pre-modern art converge with the highest ideals of twentieth-century abstraction.

Fujimura refers us to Simone Weil's notion of "attention," a habitual activity that bridges the intellectual and the spiritual. In her *Reflections on the Good Usage of School Studies,* Weil writes:

Attention consists in suspending thought, in leaving it

available, empty and sub-
ject to penetration by the
object. Our thought must
be, with regard to all the
already formed specific
thoughts, like a man on a
mountain who, looking in
front of him, sees without
looking at them many for-
ests and plains below him.
And especially, thought
must remain empty, await-
ing, not seeking anything,
but ready to receive in its
naked truth the object that
will penetrate it.

The habit of viewing art can
foster the attentiveness that
Weil praises, precisely because,
as Rouault noted, the eyes are
"the doors of the spirit." But we
must be taught by the art how to view it in this way.

Such a conception of the source and the impact of art cuts against
the grain of the dominant conceptions of art in our culture. It cuts against
the understanding of art as arbitrary self-expression. Anticipating
in certain respects a thesis of T. S. Eliot, Rouault urged that the
artist "should disappear behind his work." Of course, this does not entail,

Rouault *Reine de Cirque (au Turba . . .)*. 18.8 x 12.4 inches.
Rouault *Mademoiselle Pointu*. 11.8 x 7.6 inches.

at least for Rouault, that artists do not have distinctive styles and or attend to individual themes. It does mean that the artist must practice a certain form of self-effacing humility before his work. It also cuts against the construal of the viewer as a consumer who bestows value on the work by expressing an already formed preference.

The reduction of art to market forces of mere self-expression and consumer preference renders the work an idol that gives back to us only what we have already put into it. That is the assessment of the contemporary French philosopher Jean-Luc Marion, an assessment that resonates with Fujimura's objection to the "pollution" of our culture through "self-aggrandizement and a type of embezzlement made in the name of advancing the creative arts." In *The Crossing of the Visible,* Marion argues that the alternative to the artistic idol is the icon. Iconic art, according to Marion, simultaneously makes "visible what would otherwise remain invisible" and points beyond itself to an encounter with what remains invisible. The unsettling mixture of presence and absence in iconic painting issues a kind of call to the viewer; it seeks to engage,

43

expand, and transform the vision of the viewer.

What emerges is neither classical nor postmodern, but rather a claim that the best expressions of individual talent occur in and through a living tradition. As William Dyrness crisply puts it, "In a sense both Fujimura and Rouault demonstrate that the highest form of self-expression is to be had through the embrace of a tradition, that is both open to the future and to God, and that shows a healthy

Rouault *Je suis belle o mortels.* 16.7 x 13.5 inches.
Fujimura *La fin au-dela #4.* 9 x 12 inches.

respect for its materials." Such art invites viewers to contemplation and dialogue.

Art rooted in and fostering spiritual exercises (Weil's habit of attention) is the shared vision of Rouault and Fujimura. A reviewer of a previous Fujimura exhibit notes the way the "artist animates the color field with a central gestural form drawn by repeated calligraphic brushstrokes, evoking the cryptic narrative of an ink painting or a classical landscape scroll." Fujimura's description of his work aptly captures the visual effect: "As the light becomes trapped within pigments, a 'grace arena' is created, as the light is broken, and trapped in refraction. Yet my gestures are limited, contained, and gravity pulls the pigments like a friend."

Such a vision of art allows any individual work of art to be at once particular and universal, personal and shared. Such art can meet the demands of the five-hundred-year question: to craft works at once of this time and place and for the ages.

Hope in Exile

To aspire to discern the universal in the particular, and to attend simultaneously to the distinctive issues of the time and to eternal questions, might seem an impossible task. It seems especially quixotic in the wake of a certain strain of modernism that celebrates angst, negation, and despair. In his recently published *Modernism: The Lure of Heresy,* the renowned

Rouault *Automne versailles*
Fujimura *La fin au-dela #6.* 6 x 8 inches.

historian Peter Gay defines that late-nineteenth and twentieth-century movement in terms of heterodoxy and the practice of "principled self-scrutiny." The activity of self-scrutiny expresses itself in stylistic experimentation, in the depiction of anxiety, and in the negation of purported claims to truth, order, and beauty.

Given such assumptions, the art of Rouault eludes classification. As we noted above, some of his contemporaries accused Rouault of wallowing in the ugly and the despicable. His style is often rough, even coarse. His vibrant use of color and his penchant for abstraction, for shapes whose juxtaposition violates classic rules of perspective, call to mind the works of Cézanne and Matisse, even as his subject matter recalls Toulouse-Lautrec. While Rouault eschewed moralistic explanations of his art, he did not advocate amorality or immorality.

46 Art is not about imposing a moral vision, but rather about seeing clearly and depicting what one sees—in this case, what is in fact grotesque, degraded, and demoralized. Rouault turns to the line from Virgil's *Aeneid* where Aeneas encounters Carthaginian temple images of the fall of Troy and sadly exclaims, *"Sunt lacrimae rerum et mentem mortalia tangunt"* ("There are tears of things and mortal matters touch the mind"). The artist, according to Rouault, needs a "great faith in the midst of indifference and hostility."

What unites Aeneas with the marginalized characters populating Rouault's works is the experience of devastating and irrevocable loss. The sense of civilization in crisis, the sense of loss, and the longing to recover, if not the past, at least a way of going forward. What we need, as Maritain has written, is a "transfigurative" realism, a realism that discounts neither the pervasive sense of alienation nor the temptations to despair. In a stirring assessment, Fujimura insists that the "hell of

47

the artistic imagination" is the "only real point of departure" for artistic creation today.

If Rouault finds the hell of the imagination in the real-world degradation of prostitutes, the sorrow of clowns, and the hypocrisy of judges, Fujimura has been transfixed by the real-world hell that "opened up" on September 11, 2001, three blocks from his home, at Ground Zero in Lower Manhattan—a horror that eclipsed the artificially constructed

Fujimura *La Fin au-dela #3*. 9 x 12 inches.

nightmares of our popular films and our shock art. Faced with that horror, an honest artist should find it impossible to indulge in playful protest. Instead, contemporary nightmares can recall the artist to a perpetual calling, to articulate the "language of hope in exile."

"Hope in exile" is an apt description of the work of Rouault, his dialogue between secular and sacred, his attempt to speak the Word of the Lord in exile. His focus on the life and image of Christ presents a "true icon" of the invisible God. His art, particularly many of his landscapes, inscribes Christ into the natural order even as it inscribes the suffering of the human race into the Passion. The soliloquy thereby opens out not just to a dialogue with others but also to a silent receptivity to the One who knows us better than we know ourselves. Thus does he recover the original notion of soliloquy from Augustine; for him it is ultimately a dialogue of the soul with God. The internal search culminates in a self-discovery that coincides with the discovery of God, the Voice nearer to us than we are to ourselves. In this way, art, operating in harmony with faith, perfects the craft in unanticipated ways. Maritain's comments about Rouault apply also to Fujimura's work: "Through the inspiration of his faith, and of the contemplative promptings which are its hidden treasure, that the abiding poetry, the flash of poetic intuition . . . have reached full freedom and full scope."

48

Rouault *Crucifixion.* 19.3125 x 12.25 inches.

Augustine, *Soliloquies*, trans. Michael Foley (Notre Dame, Ind.: University of Notre Dame Press, forthcoming).

Leon Bloy, *L'Invendable* (Paris: Mercure de France, 1919).

Pierre Courthion, Rouault (New York: Harry N. Abrams Publishers, 1977).

William A. Dyrness, *Rouault: A Vision of Suffering and Salvation* (Grand Rapids, Mich: Eerdmans, 1971).

T.S. Eliot, "Tradition and the Individual Talent," in *Selected Essays* (New York: Harcourt, Brace, and Company, 1932).

Holly Flora and Soo Yun Kang, *This Anguished World of Shadows: George Rouault's Miserere et Guerre* (London: D. Giles Ltd., 2006).

Makoto Fujimura, "Abstraction and the Christian Faith," in *CIVA Newsletter* (November 1997).

Fujimura, *Refractions: A Journey of Faith, Art, and Culture*, foreword by Tim Keller (Colorado Springs, Colo.: NavPress, 2009).

Makoto Fujimura, "That Final Dance: Essay on Form and Content," in *It Was Good: Making Art to the Glory of God* (Baltimore: Square Halo Books, 2006).

Peter Gay, *Modernism: The Lure of Heresy, from Baudelaire to Beckett and Beyond* (New York: W. W. Norton & Company, 2008).

Etienne Gilson, *Painting and Reality* (New York: World Meridian Books, 1959).

E. H. Gombrich, *The Story of Art* (Englewood Cliffs, N.J.: Prentice Hall, 1995).

Soo Yun Kang, *Rouault in Perspective* (International Scholars Publishing, 2000).

Alasdair MacIntyre, *After Virtue*, third edition (Notre Dame, Ind.: University of Notre Dame Press, 2007).

Macintyre, *Whose Justice? Which Rationality?* (Notre Dame, Ind.: University of Notre Dame Press, 1989).

Jean-Luc Marion, *The Crossing of the Visible*, trans. James K. A. Smith (Palo Alto, Calif.: Stanford University Press, 2004).

Jacques Maritain, *Rouault—The Pocket Library of Great Art* (New York: Abrams Art Books, 1954).

James Romaine, *Objects of Grace: Conversations on Creativity and Faith* (Baltimore: Square Halo Books, 2002).

Georges Rouault, *Soliloquies* (Neuchatel, France: Ides et Calendes, 1944).

Jean-Marie Teze, "Action Painting," in *Mystic Masque: Semblance and Reality in Georges Rouault 1871-1958*, ed. Stephen Schloesser (Chestnut Hill, Mass.: McMullen Museum of Art, Boston College, 2008).

Richard Toben, review of Makoto Fujimura exhibit "Gravity and Grace" at The Bellas Artes Gallery, in *THE Magazine* (September 2002).

Calvin Tomkins, *The Art World, "Total Abstraction,"* in *The New Yorker* (March 25, 1996, p. 92).

Simone Weil, *Simone Weil: Modern Spiritual Masters*, ed. with introduction by Eric O. Springsted (Maryknoll, N. Y.: Orbis Books, 1998).

Simone Weil, *Waiting for God* (New York: Harper Perennial Classics, 2001).

Georges Rouault: the first Twenty-First Century Artist

A REFRACTION BY MAKOTO FUJIMURA

"No, back then this area was not very popular among artists."

I had asked Rouault's grandson Gilles if Gare de Lyon was a popular area for artists to live, having just walked about the gentrified "creative zone" nearby, filled with design studios, art students, and cafes.

No, what you see now, and what must have been seen then from Rouault's studio, are scenes of ordinary people mingled about in a theatre of life. And we should expect Georges Rouault to live where no other artists would live. His work and his life seem distinct from the conventional creative forces of the time. Picasso, Braques, Matisse, and others would have walked about the streets of Paris then, as well as Cézanne—if the light of Provence in southern France had not lured him back.

Georges Rouault (1871–1958) was a keen observer of people, and he must have enjoyed watching the square from his window. He painted figures and portraits as "a fit object of grace, while more visibly born in and for suffering."[1] He sought out the marginalized poor, prostitutes, clowns, and politicians; to him, kings and the homeless were equally significant as his symbol of brokenness. But ultimately they, especially the misfits, were celebrated as God's chosen manifestation of light into darkness.

52

Rouault was born in the wake of the Franco-Prussian War during La Commune de Paris. As the French casualties mounted, and with no hospital to go to, his mother gave birth to him by herself in the basement shelter. Georges later recounted, "I believe…that in the context of the massacres, fires and horrors, I have retained (from the cellar in which I was born) in my eyes and in my mind the fleeting matter which good fire fixes and incrusts."[2]

His early memories included being taken to the Victor Hugo state funeral march in Paris when he was 14. His "Ground Zero" began at the cellar of his Belleville home, and expanded as he saw the devastation and the fragmentation of his homeland that would confront him then, and haunt him later as France faced the shadows of Nazi invasion, and then the ideological fragmentation that the modernist intellectual milieu would engender for the remainder of his life.

He never felt comfortable in such a schism, struggling with depression: the darkness or the broken realities would insist upon him to depict the oppressiveness as is, making some of his early paintings almost unbearable. But eventually his palette would find colors streaking through the somber darkness via the clown's faces and the blemishes on the cheeks of the prostitutes. They were becoming his existential statement, as if to force back the darkness, or perhaps more accurately to give grace a chance to shine in the margins of stark and bold lines. Early on, he found refuge in the colors of the stained-glass windows he apprenticed to create, and in the prints that his grandfather, a postal worker, showed him of Manet and Rembrandt from Paris market.

In turn, today, Rouault has influenced many. As a student in Tokyo, I once asked a Zen master of calligraphy who he admired the most among the Western masters. He replied, "Georges Rouault, because his lines contain the weight of life." And in many conversations among artists and intellectuals, especially in Japan, Rouault's name pops up as a major influence. Recently I had the privilege of spending time with contemporary American great Chuck Close,[3] and he told me of his high admiration for Rouault. "I wanted to buy one of Rouault's prints as a student at Yale," he said, "but just could not afford it." For an art student to even consider buying a piece of artwork would be the greatest show of admiration.

With such a respected following among artists, one would think that Rouault would be positioned among greats such as Picasso, or perhaps Matisse, who was a close friend of Georges. But his reputation never found such foothold, as he continues to confound the critics, never seeming to fit into the neat categories of Modernists, abstract

Expressionism, or—despite exhibiting with them—the Fauves.

Why? Rouault's paintings are not ideologically driven, like the Modernists, or of pure abstraction like some of the Expressionists, or hedonistic, like the Fauves. His paintings are faithful depictions of the broken realities of his time, eloquent testimonies of color in fragmentation, and graceful reminders of faith in an agnostic and increasingly atheistic era.

Georges Rouault's paintings are a portal that peeks into ages past, and then, magically, invites us into a journey toward our future. They transport us to a past beyond the fragmentation of Modernism into the enchantment and mysteries of a medieval aesthetic, before rationality was segregated from passion and our hearts divorced from faith.

Like the stained-glass windows, for whose colors he grew to have a "passionate taste,"[4] Rouault's world is principally determined by colorist space and not dependent upon traditional formulae of illusionistic space. They create in-between space within layers of paint—what contemporary art historian James Romaine called "Grace arenas."[5] They are more than Modernist or Classical. Rouault's paintings are "Trans-Modern paintings,[6] "synthesizing bold and calligraphic colors, humble view of humanity, and a prophetic visage of a forgotten reality."

54

Like the Rembrandts he valued and imitated as a youth, and the Cézanne he celebrated in his letters and poems, Rouault paintings capture not a mere reflective, descriptive light, but Light behind the light, Reality behind reality. They are generative and seem to grow more and more pregnant as they age. Rouault may yet prove to be the first twenty-first-century painter, bringing synthesis out of an age of fragmentation. They stand in complete contrast to the path the other

Modernist artists took, like Picasso and Mondrian, to delineate and dissect reality into flat cerebral spaces. Takashi Murakami states in his "Superflat" essay that flatness is the essence of artistic innovation of recent past, considering "Superflat" an "-ism, like Cubism, Surrealism, Minimalism and Simulationism."[7] Rouault's work was a resistance to this age of "flattened perceptions."

The assumption in "Superflat" is that reality is readable in a flattened perception; Rouault spent his entire life and career disputing this idea: "Superflatism" assumes we can lose dimensionality without much harm. But as the twentieth century moved toward the collapse of form and ideas, we lost connection with the fully orbed dimensional reality. Into that increasingly flat world, Rouault gives flesh to the synthesis of these alienated elements.

When Modernism depicted chasms of splintered conditions, Rouault's little paintings shed light into that room. When the prevailing notion of existentialism posted "No Exit" signs in our studios, Rouault was a little window that looked out into a vision of wholeness. His work awakens us to a greater sensation.

Yet to me as a graduate student, Rouault's window was closed. I felt the oppression of "No Exit" reality. For a modern painter, one of the few avenues left for me to explore was the language of angst and despair. Very similar to Rouault's depiction of his darker images early on, I began to depict sinister elements of nature.

It was then that I encountered the works of Rouault's Passion paintings at The Bridgestone Museum and other Rouault paintings at Idemitsu Museum in Tokyo. The Japanese, for surprising reasons, have the best collection of Rouault. The postwar intellectual movement of Shirakaba championed artists like Rouault along with other continental artists. I made pilgrimages to see these small but heavily painted surfaces.

Once in my graduate program studio in Tokyo, one of the assistant professors walked into the studio unannounced. I was working on a semi-abstract painting that I felt was close to being finished. He took one look at the painting and said, "This painting is so beautiful, it's almost terrifying," and walked out. Immediately I proceeded to wash the painting down, destroying the surface.

Why did I do that? It was because I realized, in honesty, I did not have a room for that kind of beauty inside my heart. Only now do I realize it may have been Rouault's paintings that caused me to pursue the path of "terrible beauty," a path I was not prepared to walk. I was simply astounded that this terrible beauty would be birthed out of my own hands. Philosophically, I did not have the luxury of beauty having captured and possessed my heart.

56

Jacques Maritain's writings began to affect my philosophical outlook then. Since college I had carried around his seminal work *Creative Intuitions in Art and Poetry.* In that book Maritain wrote "For poetry there is no goal, no specifying end. But there is an end beyond. Beauty is the necessary correlative and end beyond any end of poetry."[7] Beauty as a "necessary correlative" of art and poetry, allows for a broader context in which deeper wrestling, and synthesis, can take place. Only in reading up on Rouault's life for this exhibit did I discover that Maritain wrote *Creative Intuitions* as a summarization of his encounter and friendship with Rouault. Little did I know of this Thomist thinker's overlap with Rouault. It could very well be that while my visual arena was touched by Rouault's "weight of life" paintings, I was concurrently being influenced philosophically by Maritain, without knowing the connection between the two. And it occurs to me now that I may not have encountered Rouault, and perhaps Maritain, to such an extent if I did not come to Japan.

Thus, Rouault's influence in my life is far more than mere inspiration; he gave permission in the "No Exit" room to look outside from the most unlikely place of exile. His paintings were little windows into a Reality I did not know existed. What I saw there was both beautiful and terrifying. It showed a path of a suffering servant who took on the broken condition of our souls, the historic Jesus of Nazareth, who chose to walk into darkness claiming to be the "light of the world." The images of the Savior that entered my eyes, became etched into my heart, and eventually broke through into my life. They became, along with the words of William Blake and Jacques Maritain, central guiding posts for my journey of art, faith, and creativity.[8]

In Rouault's sunlit studio, I faced a photo showing stacks of paintings. The varnish bottles and used bristles of brushes seemed to beckon the master artist to walk in and start working. The heavy impasto of his surfaces, though now completely dry, gave the illusion that it had been painted yesterday, still giving the illusion of a slight scent of linseed oil. The tubes of paint lay inside the boxes they came in, somewhat arranged in an ad hoc manner. His process of working allowed parallel progression, and he literally stacked framed paintings on top of each other, working in literal layers. One painting competed against, and even visually bled into, another.

The colors Rouault utilized are combinations I was taught to avoid in school. Bright yellow and sharp purple never should work well on a painting, nor muted color mixed with black, and yet in Rouault's hands, these "impossible" colors speak deeply and resonate. To observe each painting of Rouault is to throw away conventions of painting, to watch a literal miracle take place in front of you. This is why to this day, many painters admire him and see him as their great influence.

58

Rouault was a painter's painter; purists gravitate toward his work. What makes him different from Picasso, Matisse, Bonnard, or countless other example of artists from around the same period? Is it the use of colors? Application of paint? Delineation of lines? Rouault's works are unique in their audacity of conviction: an affirmation of the light that lies behind the darkness, and the gestural authority to capture that reality. His works still, so many years after the viscous layers of paint have dried out, teach us to *trust* paint. Rouault reminds us that our souls are being squeezed out like fresh paint directly onto the canvas of modern struggles—raw, pungent, and pure, about to be pushed about by a great master. And when we allow ourselves to be moved in such a way, inevitably we begin to notice the visual language Rouault developed all his life, and we may finally begin to truly "see" Rouault's paintings.

I've identified three visual "keys" that may help the reader in looking at Rouault's paintings in this book and in museums. These keys are: his approach to *perspective*, the *sun/moon* as a symbol, and his unique use of *colors*.

The masterpiece *Christ in the Outskirts* depicts Christ with two other figures. The perspective used here is much like the contemporary artist Richard Diebenkorn or Anselm Kiefer, as an "angelic" perspective. The perspective is neither perpendicular to the ground, nor from the ground looking into the horizon: the angle is "angelic," halfway between heaven and earth. Recently, at Fuchu Museum in Tokyo, I spoke in front of one of my *Twin Rivers of Tamagawa* paintings displayed there (see page 28), and I noted my unconscious use of the same perspective in my Twin Rivers paintings, imitating Rouault's work.

59

When I see the *Outskirts* painting now in the collection at Bridgestone Museum in Tokyo, my eyes gravitate up toward the moon in the sky. But then, with Rouault, the moon is not guaranteed to be just a moon. This is very similar to Vincent van Gogh's sun/moon in *Starry Night,* a symbol of the new heavens and the new earth.[9] But for Rouault, the sun/moon is a sacramental vision, like the round bread of life offered by the priest at a Mass.

In France, a large, round, golden signpost (called a monstrance) is often used in Catholic Masses to lift up the Sacramental reality, inviting the communicants to encounter worship. The Bread of Life—the body of Christ—is superimposed with the sun. In such a reality, materiality has direct connection with the sacred, and gives conviction to an artist like Rouault to see the spiritual, heavenly presence manifesting itself in the reality of earth. If a Communion wafer is for Rouault the actual body of Christ, then the intensity of the greater Reality can, in a smaller way, inhabit even ordinary paint. Heaven can, in other words, intervene in our ordinary reality to break forth physically. And this reality of heaven being manifested on earth is a portal into any earthly reality to be filled with a sacramental possibility.

During my recent stay in Japan, I traveled to Yamanashi prefecture, where Rouault's work is exhibited at Shirakaba Museum. The Rouault Chapel was designed by Yoshio Taniguchi with a crucifix that Rouault him-

1   William A. Dyrness, *Rouault: A Vision of Suffering and Salvation,* (Eerdmans, Grand Rapids, Michigan, 1971) p. 108.

2   Georges Rouault, *Correspondance [de] Georges Rouault [et] André Suarès* (Paris: Gallimard, 1960), p. 49; quoted in *Semblance and Reality in Georges Rouault, 1871–1958,* ed. Stephen Schloesser (Chicago: The University of Chicago Press, 2008), 27.

3   At the Aspen Institute, 2009.

4   Georges Rouault, Souvenirs intimes (Paris: E. Frapier, 1927), 51; quoted in Bernard Doering, "*Lacrymae rerum:* Creative Intuition of the Transapparent Reality," in *Semblance and Reality in Georges Rouault, 1871–1958,* ed. Stephen Schloesser (Chicago: The University of Chicago Press, 2008), p. 390.

5   see *Art as Prayer,* (International Arts Movement, 1999).

6   I like to thank Dr. Paul Vitz for coining this term at an IAM lecture in 1998.

7   Takashi Murakami, *Superflat* (Madra Publishing, Japan, 2000) p. 25.

8   Jacques Maritain, *Creative Intuition in Art and Poetry,The A.W. Mellon Lectures in the Fine Arts* (Meridian Books, New York, 1953) p. 131.

9   See "River Grace," an International Arts Movement publication (www.rivergrace.com).

10   See my "Refractions" essay on van Gogh, (http://makotofujimura.blogspot.com/2008/01/refractions-26-epistle-of-van-gogh.html)

Special thanks to Jean-Marie Porté for the photos in this Refraction.

Other books featuring Makoto Fujimura

IT WAS GOOD: MAKING ART TO THE GLORY OF GOD

"*It Was Good* is one of the best examples I know of the new day that is dawning in Christian conversation on the arts. What we have needed is a thick description both of Christianity and of art making. And both are here in abundance, along with generous displays of great art motivated by faith both from the present and the past."
—*William Dyrness, author of* Rouault: A Vision of Suffering and Salvation

OBJECTS OF GRACE: CONVERSATIONS ON CREATIVITY AND FAITH

"[A] colorful and concise collection of interviews and art from some of America's most intriguing Christian artists. [James] Romaine interviews ten artists, presenting color reproductions of the artists' work along with the text of the interviews. Each artist dialogues on what it means for a Christian to engage in the creating process." —*Image: A Journal of the Arts and Religion*